KID CHEFS

# COOKING WITH PASTA

Rose Miles

Enslow PUBLISHING

Please visit our website, www.enslow.com. For a free color catalog of all our high-quality books, call toll free 1-800-398-2504 or fax 1-877-980-4454



Published in 2027 by
**Enslow Publishing**
2544 Clinton Street
Buffalo, NY 14224



Portions of this work were originally authored by Kristen Rajczak and published as *Ingredients for a Healthy Life: Perfect Pasta Recipes*. All new material in this edition is authored by Rose Miles.



Cataloging-in-Publication Data
Names: Miles, Rose.
Title: Cooking with pasta / Rose Miles.
Description: Buffalo, NY : Enslow Publishing, 2027. | Series: Kid chefs | Includes glossary and index.
Identifiers: ISBN 9781978548602 (pbk.) | ISBN 9781978548619 (library bound) | ISBN 9781978548626 (ebook)
Subjects: LCSH: Cooking (Pasta)--Juvenile literature. | Pasta products--Juvenile literature.
Classification: LCC TX809.M17 M674 2027 | DDC 641.822--dc23

Printed in China

Photos Credits: Cover, p. 1 totsaporn/Shutterstock.com; cover, p. 1 nelea33/Shutterstock.com; cover, p. 1 JeniFoto/Shutterstock.com; cover, p. 1 Peter Hermes Furian/Shutterstock.com; cover, p. 1 Tatiana Volgutova/Shutterstock.com; p. 4, 6, 8, 10, 12, 14, 16, 19 ricorico/Shutterstock.com; p. 5 PeopleImages/Shutterstock.com; p. 6 Kingarion/Shutterstock.com; p. 7 kungfu01/Shutterstock.com; p. 8 ZayacSK/Shutterstock.com; p. 9 Elena Shashkina/Shutterstock.com; p. 10 mernk/Shutterstock.com; p. 11 New Africa/Shutterstock.com; p. 13 nelea33/Shutterstock.com; p. 14 OnlyFOOD/Shutterstock.com; p. 15 ndsign/Shutterstock.com; p. 17 JeniFoto/Shutterstock.com; p. 19 Pixel-Shot/Shutterstock.com; p. 20 New Africa/Shutterstock.com; p. 21 Littlekidmoment/Shutterstock.com

CPSIA compliance information: Batch #QSENS27: For further information, contact Enslow Publishing, New York, New York, at 1-800-398-2504.

# Contents



Recipes in this book may use knives, mixers, and hot stove tops. Ask for an adult's help when using these tools.

Words in the glossary appear in **bold** type the first time they are used in the text.

# It's Pasta!

In the United States, pasta is commonly thought of as Italian **cuisine**. We most often prepare it in the Italian style, boiled in water and served with tomato sauce. But it can be tossed with just about any meat, sauce, and vegetable.

Pasta dough is a simple combination of flour and water or eggs. The same ingredients are used to make similar dough in **cultures** around the world! In Poland, there's pierogi (puh-ROH-gee). Germans and Hungarians eat spaetzle (SHPEHT-sluh). Orzo is common in Greece.

## Do You Have Allergies?

The **recipes** in this book may use **ingredients** that contain or have come into contact with nuts, gluten, dairy products, and other common causes of **allergies**. If you have any food allergies, please ask a parent or teacher for help when cooking and tasting!

Pasta is inexpensive and easy to make. It's a popular dinner choice!

# Pasta Throughout History

Though it's hard to say where pasta was first made, we do know it's been around for thousands of years. **Archaeologists** think central Asia was a likely place for the creation of the first noodles. In the 8th century, the Arab people took over the part of Europe that's now Italy, probably introducing pasta to that area.

It wasn't until the mid-1800s that southern Italian cooks began pairing tomatoes and pasta. Now, one of the most popular ways to serve pasta is with tomato sauce!

### Tasty Tidbits

When tomatoes first arrived from the Americas, Europeans thought they were poisonous. They're nightshades, a plant family that does have some poisonous members!

# Homemade Spaghetti Sauce

makes 6 servings

## Ingredients:

1 tablespoon olive oil
1 medium onion, finely chopped
2 cloves garlic, minced
2 (28-ounce) cans whole tomatoes, drained and chopped
3 tablespoons tomato paste
1 teaspoon dried oregano
1 bay leaf
Salt and pepper

## Directions:

1. Heat olive oil in a large pot on the stove top on medium-low heat. Add the onion and cook for about 5 minutes, stirring it a few times.
2. Mix in the garlic and cook for about 2 minutes.
3. Add the canned tomatoes, tomato paste, oregano, bay leaf, and a pinch of salt and pepper. Cook on low for about 30 minutes, uncovered. The sauce will thicken.
4. If you like a smoother sauce, allow the sauce to cool and use a blender or food processor to break down the tomato chunks.
5. Serve over pasta.

*Skip the store-bought jars! Make this easy, tasty sauce to serve atop your favorite pasta.*

# Around the World

By the 1300s, dried pastas were circling the globe. They lasted a long time before being cooked and so made good stores aboard ships.

Pasta first came to the Americas with Spanish settlers in the 1500s. In the late 1700s, Thomas Jefferson brought two cases of macaroni back to the United States when he returned from Paris, France. But it was the arrival of Italian **immigrants** in the late 1800s that truly began the pasta craze in the United States.

### Tasty Tidbits

When pasta reached the area around the Mediterranean Sea, durum wheat began to be the major flour used to make pasta, just as it is today.

# Pizza Spaghetti

Would you rather have spaghetti or pizza? With this dish, you can have both!

makes about 8 servings

## Ingredients:

1 (8-ounce) package spaghetti, broken into 2-inch pieces
1 egg
¼ cup milk
2 cups shredded, low-fat mozzarella cheese
¼ teaspoon salt
¼ teaspoon garlic salt
1 (16-ounce) jar spaghetti sauce
1 teaspoon dried oregano
¼ teaspoon dried basil
pizza toppings (sliced pepperoni, peppers, pineapple, etc.)

## Directions:

1. Preheat oven to 425 degrees.
2. Fill a pot with water and bring it to a boil on the stove top. Add the spaghetti and cook for about 10 minutes. Drain the pasta in a **colander**.
3. Beat the egg in a bowl. Mix in milk, ½ cup of the mozzarella cheese, salt, and garlic salt. Stir in the spaghetti.
4. Prepare a baking dish with cooking spray. Spread the spaghetti mixture evenly in the bottom. This will be the "crust."

5. Bake for 15 minutes.
6. Take the "crust" out of the oven, and reduce the oven temperature to 350 degrees.
7. Spread sauce on the crust. Add the rest of the cheese and sprinkle with the oregano and basil. Top with your favorite pizza toppings.
8. Bake for 30 minutes. Allow the pizza to cool for 5 minutes before cutting.

# Where Does Pasta Come From?

Dried pasta is quick and cheap to buy at the grocery store. But some people make it by hand.

First, semolina—the flour made from durum wheat—is carefully mixed with warm water or eggs. It's **kneaded** for several minutes and left to rest. Next, the dough is rolled out and put through a pasta machine, which stretches the dough to the needed thickness. The pasta is then cut into ribbons or shapes and cooked or frozen. It takes extra time to make homemade pasta, but the taste is worth it!

### Tasty Tidbits

Pasta made in a factory is made in much the same way as homemade pasta, just on a larger scale. In addition, shapes—such as the popular elbow macaroni—can be made using molds and sheets with holes in them.

*Making homemade pasta is a fun and tasty activity!*

# Perfect Pastas

Spaghetti and tomato sauce is a classic pairing. Here are a few other types of pasta and some of the best ways to serve them.

Angel hair pasta is very thin, so it goes best with light or creamy sauces. The delicate strands have a light and airy feel.

Manicotti noodles are long, wide tubes. They are often stuffed with cheese and meat and then baked.

Ravioli and tortellini are stuffed pastas. They may hold meat, **pureed** (pyuh-RAYD) vegetables, or cheese. They can be cooked in soups, served with tomato sauce, or just tossed with a little garlic and olive oil for a tasty and filling meal.

### Tasty Tidbits

Fettuccine is another popular pasta. It's egg pasta that looks like thicker, flat spaghetti. Fettuccine is often served with cream sauces.

# Mexican-Style Lasagna

## Ingredients:

makes 4 servings

¾ cup salsa from a jar
1 ½ teaspoons cumin
1 (14.5-ounce) can no-salt-added diced tomatoes
1 (8-ounce) can no-salt-added tomato sauce
6 precooked lasagna noodles
1 cup frozen whole-kernel corn, thawed
1 (15-ounce) can black beans, rinsed and drained
2 cups shredded, low-fat Mexican-blend cheese
¼ cup chopped green onions

*Try this yummy twist to traditional lasagna recipes. If you like spicy food, add some jalapeños to the top!*

## Directions:

1. Preheat oven to 450 degrees.
2. Mix together salsa, cumin, diced tomatoes, and tomato sauce. Spray a small, square baking dish with cooking spray, and spread about ⅔ cup of the sauce in the bottom.
3. Place two of the noodles over the sauce.
4. Top the noodles with about ½ cup each of the corn and beans. Sprinkle with about ½ cup of cheese, followed by another ⅔ cup of sauce.
5. Make another layer in the same way.
6. Top with the last two noodles. Cover the noodles with the remaining sauce, then the rest of the cheese.
7. Cover with tin foil. Bake for about 30 minutes.
8. Before serving, sprinkle the onions on top.

# Health Benefits

Pasta is a good source of some **nutrients**, including vitamin A, which helps keep your eyes, skin, and bones healthy. Pasta also provides carbohydrates, the main nutrient your body uses for energy. Pasta can be a great part of your **diet** when paired with vegetables and protein.

Whole-wheat pasta is an even better choice for your body! It has fiber and protein. An easy way to introduce your family to whole-wheat pasta is by replacing half of the regular pasta in a recipe with whole-wheat. Slowly increase the amount until all your pasta is whole-wheat!

### Tasty Tidbits

Traditional pastas don't have a lot of fiber and protein because the parts of wheat that have these nutrients are removed before the flour is ground.

# Mac and Cheese

## Ingredients:

makes 4 servings

1 ¼ cups uncooked whole-wheat elbow macaroni
1 cup 1 percent milk
2 tablespoons all-purpose flour
1 ¼ cups shredded, low-fat sharp cheddar cheese
½ teaspoon salt
½ teaspoon pepper
1 ¼ cups whole-wheat breadcrumbs
1 tablespoon butter, melted

*Pump up the healthfulness of this recipe by mixing in some broccoli, peas, or zucchini. Veggies taste great with pasta and cheese!*

## Directions:

1. Cook the macaroni by following the directions on the box. Drain it well.
2. Heat a medium-sized pan on the stove top on medium heat. Mix together milk and flour in the pan for about 2 minutes or until thick.
3. Add cheese, salt, and pepper, stirring with a fork or whisk until smooth.
4. Stir in pasta and coat with the cheese mixture. Turn the heat off, cover, and let stand for 4 minutes.
5. Heat a skillet on the stove top and lightly toast breadcrumbs for about 5 minutes, stirring a few times. Add melted butter and mix together.
6. After about 2 minutes, remove the skillet from heat and sprinkle the breadcrumb and butter mixture over the macaroni. Serve right away.

# Balanced Meals

Pasta is delicious, and it's easy to eat too much. It's often hard to figure out the right amount of pasta to put on your plate. A good rule is to give yourself a helping of cooked pasta about the size of your fist. For many people, that ends up being between ¾ cup and 1 cup of cooked pasta.

Pasta is just one part of a balanced meal. If you divide up your plate, about half should be covered in veggies. The other half of your plate should be divided between the pasta and a protein, such as chicken or fish.

*Orzo looks like rice, but it's actually pasta! This recipe calls for lots of veggies to fill you up without eating too much pasta.*

**Tasty Tidbits**

There aren't a lot of health concerns about pasta itself, especially if you choose whole-wheat. The problem lies in how much pasta you eat!

# Veggie-Filled Orzo Salad

## Ingredients:

makes 4 servings

Salad:

1 cup uncooked whole-wheat orzo

9 asparagus stalks, trimmed and cut into 1-inch pieces

1 head broccoli, cut into small trees

1 handful cilantro, chopped

1 handful alfalfa sprouts

⅓ cup almonds, chopped and toasted

½ of a small cucumber, chopped

1 avocado, sliced

¼ cup crumbled feta cheese

Dressing:

1 clove garlic, mashed and minced

1 pinch salt

2 tablespoons fresh lemon juice

¼ cup extra-virgin olive oil

## Directions:

1. Fill a large pot with water and bring it to a boil on the stove top. Add orzo and cook according to the package directions. The pasta should be cooked without being mushy.
2. Just before the orzo is done, stir the asparagus and broccoli into the boiling water. Allow the vegetables to cook for about 30 seconds.
3. Remove the pan from the heat, and pour the pasta and vegetables into a colander to drain. Run cold water over them for about 2 minutes to stop them from cooking more.
4. In a small bowl, combine the garlic, lemon juice, extra-virgin olive oil, and salt.
5. Toss the orzo, broccoli, asparagus, and cilantro with about half the dressing.
6. Add the sprouts, almonds, cucumber, avocado, and feta cheese. Toss gently. Serve immediately or refrigerate. Add more dressing as needed.

# Plenty to Choose From

Today, nontraditional pastas are easy to find in many grocery stores. You can often find pasta made of spelt and buckwheat flours, two tasty grains. But some pastas don't use grains at all. Lentil pasta has an earthy flavor, which goes well with a roasted vegetable sauce. Almond flour pasta has a nutty flavor. Black bean pasta has lots of protein and fiber—and it's black!

Brown rice and quinoa (KEEN-wah) pastas have become a common choice for people with celiac disease. Their bodies react badly to gluten, a protein found in wheat and some other grains. Regular pasta would make them feel quite sick. Gluten-free pastas are made for people who follow a certain diet or just want to try something new.

There are lots of pasta options to change up the tastes and textures of your favorite meals.

## Tasty Tidbits

Gnocchi (NYO-kee) is chewy pasta made from potatoes. Though it's filling and hearty on its own, gnocchi is commonly served with thicker sauces. A little butter can also go a long way on a plate of gnocchi!

# Time to Cook!

Get creative! Now that you know all about pasta, it's time to experiment in the kitchen. You could try tossing rigatoni with some peas and pesto, a sauce made with basil and garlic. You could serve cold Asian noodles and steamed broccoli with a drizzle of a nutty sauce made by mixing ¼ cup soy sauce, 1 tablespoon peanut butter, and ½ teaspoon ginger. Or, you could cook up some Polish pierogi in a frying pan with a little butter and a chopped-up onion. Yum!

Making your own pasta is a really fun way to spend an afternoon. Ask an adult to help you find everything you need!

*With pasta, the possibilities are endless!*

# Why Eat Pasta?

## Pasta Provides Nutrients

- Vitamin A keeps skin, bones, and eyes healthy. Potassium helps your heart and muscles work well.

## Pasta Fills You Up

- Whole-wheat pasta is a good source of fiber, which keeps your digestive system working well. And because fiber makes us feel full, eating pasta can stop us from eating too much junk food.

## Pasta Makes You Strong

- The protein in whole-wheat pasta helps build and repair muscles.

## Pasta Boosts Energy

- The carbohydrates in whole-wheat pasta give the body energy, so you can get out there to run and play!

# Glossary

**allergy:** a body's sensitivity to usually harmless things in the surroundings, such as dust, pollen, or mold

**archaeologist:** a scientist who studies ancient buildings and objects to learn about past human life and activities

**colander:** a bowl with small holes used for washing or draining food

**cuisine:** a style of cooking

**culture:** the beliefs and ways of life of a group of people

**diet:** the food one usually eats

**immigrant:** one who comes to a new country to settle there

**ingredient:** a food that is mixed with other foods

**knead:** to work with dough until it's smooth

**nutrient:** something a living thing needs to grow and stay alive

**puree:** to grind or blend cooked food into a thick paste or liquid. Also, the paste or liquid itself.

**recipe:** an explanation of how to make food

# Fact Check

1. In the United States, pasta is commonly thought of as______ cuisine.
   a. Polish
   b. German
   c. Italian

2. Which vitamin helps keep your eyes, skin, and bones healthy?
   a. vitamin A
   b. potassium
   c. vitamin C

3. About _____________of cooked pasta is a good serving size.
   a. 1 cup
   b. 2 cups
   c. a plate-full

Answers: 1. c, 2. a, 3. a

# On the Internet

**Fresh Homemade Pasta, Made Simply**
*https://thekidshouldseethis.com/post/fresh-homemade-pasta-made-simply-recipe*
Watch this video to learn how to make a simple pasta using a pasta machine.

**Share the Pasta**
*https://sharethepasta.org/*
Check out pasta recipes and tips. Then, test your pasta knowledge!

**Publisher's note to educators and parents:** Our editors have carefully reviewed these websites to ensure that they are suitable for students. Many websites change frequently, however, and we cannot guarantee that a site's future contents will continue to meet our high standards of quality and educational value. Be advised that students should be closely supervised whenever they access the Internet.

# Index